DEVELOPING
the LEADERS
AROUND YOU

JOHN C. MAXWELL

DEVELOPING the LEADERS AROUND YOU

How *to* HELP OTHERS
REACH THEIR FULL POTENTIAL

CONTENTS

LETTER FROM JOHN C. MAXWELL

Dear Friend,

Developing leaders is essential to make a great and lasting impact. The leader sees the big picture, but he or she needs other leaders to help make their mental picture a reality.

You and I are going to embark on a journey of personal growth. In this training course you will be challenged not only to learn about developing leaders but also to take the action steps necessary to invest in the potential leaders around you. You'll learn principles that have been tested and proven again and again.

The time you spend with this material will prove to be a worthy investment. Your organization will benefit as you put these ideas into practice.

I have devoted my life to equipping people, and it is my hope that you will take the *Developing the Leaders Around You* training to heart by growing and developing other leaders.

Your friend,

John C. Maxwell

John C. Maxwell

INTRODUCTION

This book is designed to emphasize what you should learn from the lessons. As you watch the lessons, take comprehensive notes in your workbook. Read *Developing the Leaders Around You* to gain an even deeper understanding of the principles being taught. In doing so, your understanding of developing other leaders will grow.

After you have completed this book, it can serve as a helpful reference guide as you consider your responsibility as a leader/team member and how to improve as you function in that role. Approach this course with the knowledge that, upon completion, you have the knowledge to help develop yourself and others into better leaders.

DEVELOPING the LEADERS AROUND YOU

SESSION 1

SESSION 1

The two most important questions that leaders ask themselves:

1. Am I developing _____ potential as a leader?

2. Am I helping _____ leaders develop their potential?

Note: Most producers are not _____ !

Why Leaders Need to Reproduce Leaders

1. The organization's growth potential is _____ _____
   to its personnel potential.

Grow the People…Grow the Organization

The Law of Explosive Growth: "To _____ Growth, Lead Followers…

                                    To _____ , Lead Leaders"

                                    —*The 21 Irrefutable Laws of Leadership*

2. Those closest to the leader will _____ the success of the leader.

The Law of the Chain: "The Strength of the Team is Impacted by its

                            Weakest Link"

                            —*The 17 Indisputable Laws of Teamwork*

$$10 + 10 + 10 + 10 + 10 = \underline{\hspace{3cm}}$$

$$10 + 10 + 10 + 10 + \ 5 = \underline{\hspace{3cm}}$$

⎫ Loss of 10%

$$10 \times 10 \times 10 \times 10 \times 10 = \underline{\hspace{3cm}}$$

$$10 \times 10 \times 10 \times 10 \times \ 5 = \underline{\hspace{3cm}}$$

⎫ Loss of 50%

My Success Journey:

1) I want to make a _____ .

2) I want to make a difference with _____ .

3) I want to make a difference with people who _____ to make a difference.

4) I want to make a difference with people who want to make a difference and who _____ make a difference.

5) I want to make a difference with people who want to make a difference and who can make a difference doing _____ that makes a difference.

3. _____ organization has a shortage of leaders.

Gallup Poll: "When people leave their organizations _____ % are actually leaving their managers."

"So much of what we call management consists in making it difficult for people to work."

—PETER DRUCKER

SESSION 1, CONTINUED

Leadership Is ...

Leadership is the courage to put oneself at risk.

Leadership is the courage to be open to new ideas.

Leadership is being dissatisfied with the current reality.

Leadership is taking responsibility while others are making excuses.

Leadership is seeing the possibilities in a situation while others are seeing the limitations.

Leadership is evoking in others the capacity to dream.

Leadership is inspiring others with a vision of what they can contribute.

Leadership is your heart speaking to the hearts of others.

Leadership is the integration of heart, head and soul.

Leadership is the power of the one made many and the many made one.

Leadership is the capacity to care, and in caring, to liberate the ideas, energy and capacities of others.

Leadership is the willingness to stand out in a crowd.

Leadership is the ability to submerge your ego for the sake of what is best.

Leadership is, above all, courageous.

Leadership is an open mind and an open heart.

Leadership is the dream made flesh.

Review:

Why Leaders Need to Reproduce Leaders

1. The organization's growth potential is directly related to its personnel potential.

2. Those closest to the leader will determine the success of the leader.

3. Every organization has a shortage of leaders.

4. Leaders attract other _____.

It takes a leader to _____ a leader.

It takes a leader to _____ a leader.

It takes a leader to _____ a leader.

The Law of Magnetism: "Who You Are is Who You Attract"

*"The growth and development of people is
the highest calling of leadership."*

—HARVEY FIRESTONE

Application

1. List five or six team members closest to you with which you lead.

_____

_____

_____

2. List the top three qualities that have drawn them to you.

_____

_____

_____

3. Are you developing them as leaders? Do you have a game plan for them? Are they growing? Have they been able to lift your load? Why?

_____

_____

_____

4. Is your organization making it a priority to develop leaders? Why or why not?

_____

_____

_____

5. What can you do in your current position to help develop leaders?

_____

_____

_____

Put into Practice

Leaders attract other leaders. Before you can lead others you must first be able to lead yourself. If you are not currently on a leadership growth path, spend some time to develop a personal growth plan that will help you to become a better leader yourself. This may include books, training tapes, magazines, etc., but create a plan that you can execute within your schedule.

DEVELOPING the LEADERS AROUND YOU

SESSION 2

SESSION 2

It's always easier to dismiss people than it is to train them. No great leader ever built a reputation on firing people. Many have built a reputation developing people.

The Leadership Challenge

Leaders are hard to _____ .

Leaders are hard to _____ .

Leaders are hard to _____ .

Leaders are hard to _____ .

The Picture of a Potential Leader

1. Leaders _____ _____ _____ _____ _____
_____ _____ .

> *"There is no future in any job.*
> *The future lies in the person who holds the job."*
> —GEORGE CRANE

Every organization has four types of people who affect momentum.

1) Momentum _____ —they say and do things that _____ momentum.

2) Momentum _____ —they say and do things that _____ momentum.

3) Momentum _____ —they say and do things that _____ momentum.

4) Momentum _____ —they say and do things that _____ momentum.

Sel not Spel

A newly hired traveling salesman wrote his first sales report to the home office. It so stunned the brass in the sales department because it was obvious that the new sales person was ignorant! Here's what he wrote:

> *"I seen this outfit which they ain't never bot a dime's worth of nothin from us and I sole them some goods. I'm now goin to Chicawgo."*

Before the man could be given the heave-ho by the sales manager, along came this letter from Chicago:

> *"I cum hear and sole them haff a millyon."*

Fearful if he did, and afraid if he didn't fire the ignorant salesman, the sales manager dumped the problem in the lap of the president. The following morning, the ivory towered sales department members were amazed to see posted on the bulletin-board-above the two letters written by the ignorant salesman-this memo from the president:

> *"We ben spending two much time trying to spel instead of tryin to sel. Let's watch those sails. I want everybody should read these letters from Gooch who is on the rode doin a grate job for us and you should go out and do like he done."*

2. Leaders _____ _____ .

Leadership is Influence!

Leaders Have Two Characteristics:

1) They are _____ somewhere.

2) They are able to _____ others to go with them.

Three Influence Questions to Ask

1) Who do they _____ ? (who is following them)

2) Who _____ _____ ? (who are they following)

3) Are they _____ or _____ influence? (past or potential leader)

Levels of Influence

Highest—　　They influence _____ .

　　　　　　They influence those _____ them.

　　　　　　They influence those _____ them.

　　　　　　They influence those _____ them.

Lowest—　　They influence _____ _____ .

A leader doesn't just see the person; he or she sees all the people that person influences.

3. Leaders _____ _____ .

"The major difference between successful and unsuccessful people is how they think."

—*THINKING FOR A CHANGE*

Leaders Are...

1) _____ _____ Thinkers

　　Leaders see _____ others see.

　　Leaders see _____ _____ others see.

2) _____ Thinkers

"The real path to greatness requires simplicity and difference."

—JIM COLLINS

3) _____ Thinkers

"No matter what you are currently able to do, creativity can make you capable of more."

The Value of Creativity? _____

4) _____ Thinkers

"The first responsibility of a leader is to define reality."

—MAX DEPREE

5) _____ Thinkers

Strategic thinking is the bridge that links where you are to where you want to be.

6) _____ Thinkers

"Nothing is so embarrassing as watching someone do something that you said could not be done."

—SAM EWING

7) _____ Thinkers

Reflective thinking turns experience into insight.

8) _____ Thinkers

"None of us is as smart as all of us."

—KEN BLANCHARD

9) _____ Thinkers

"There ain't no rules around here. We're trying to accomplish something."

—THOMAS EDISON

10) _____ Thinkers

"Learn—Earn—Return. These are the 3 phases of life."

—JACK BALOUSEK

Application

1. How would those you lead describe how well you relate to them?

_____

_____

_____

2. How accurate is your assessment of potential leaders? Are you usually mistaken, somewhat accurate, or almost always right? Why do you think so?

_____

_____

_____

3. List the members on your team and under each one list what you perceive are their top three styles of thinking based on the teaching.

_____

_____

_____

4. Based on how your team members are thinking, do you have them in the proper place where they can maximize their potential and yield the best results and growth?

_____

_____

_____

5. Who are your team members influencing?

_____

_____

_____

Put into Practice

Based on what you have learned in this session and answered in the application portion, spend significant quality time analyzing and evaluating your team. Who appears to be your best potential leaders from what you have learned? Who are they influencing, how are they thinking, are they generating momentum, etc.? Set aside time to work with these people and determine if they are individuals you could develop as a leader. This is your next step in developing leaders.

DEVELOPING the LEADERS AROUND YOU

SESSION 3

SESSION 3

Five Levels of Leadership

R_____
People follow because of who you are and what you represent

NOTE: This step is reserved for leaders who have spent years growing people and organizations. Few make it. Those who do are bigger than life.

5 P_____

NOTE: This is where long-range growth occurs. Your commitment to developing leaders will ensure ongoing growth to the organization and to people. Do whatever you can to achieve and stay on this level.

R_____
People follow because of what you have done for them

4 P_____ _____

R_____
People follow because of what you have done for the organization

NOTE: This is where success is sensed by most people. They like you and what you are doing. Problems are fixed with very little effort because of momentum.

3 P_____

2 P_____

R_____
People follow because they want to

NOTE: People will follow you beyond your stated authority. This level allows work to be fun. Caution: Staying too long on this level without rising will cause highly motivated people to become restless.

1 P_____

R_____
People follow because they have to

NOTE: Your influence will not extend beyond the lines of your job description. The longer you stay here, the higher the turnover and the lower the morale.

How People Learn

Researchers say we remember _____ % of what we hear,

_____ % of what we see,

_____ % of what we say,

_____ % of what we hear, see, say and do.

The Five Step Process for Turning Producers Into Reproducers

1. _____ _____

People _____ what people _____

Five Thoughts About Modeling

1) It is easier to _____ what is right than to _____ what is right.

"No matter what you teach the child, he insists on behaving like his parents."

Two Types of Leaders: _____ _____ _____ sends

people to their destination.

_____ _____ _____ takes people

to their destination.

{ When what I do and what I say is the same, the result is _____ . }

{ When what I do and what I say is different, the result is _____ . }

*"Nothing is more confusing than people who
give good advice and set bad examples."*

—NORMAN VINCENT PEALE

SESSION 3, CONTINUED

2) People do what people see.

Pint = Gallon: A Pint of _____ is equal to a Gallon of _____ .

How we learn: _____ % Visual

_____ % Audio

_____ % Other Senses

It takes a leader to _____ a leader.

It takes a leader to _____ a leader.

It takes a leader to _____ a leader.

3) Work on yourself _____ you work on others.

Leaders go _____ !

Questions I Ask Myself *Before* I Ask Others

1) Have I done what I am about to ask others to do?

If the answer is "yes," this gives me _____ .

2) Am I doing what I am about to ask others to do?

If the answer is "yes," this gives me _____ .

3) Am I willing to do again, what I am about to ask others to do?

If the answer is "yes," this gives me _____ .

4) Can I do well what I am asking others to do?

If the answer is "yes," this gives me _____ .

The result of answering "yes" to all 4 questions?… _____ !

4) Work on yourself _____ than you work on others.

    Most of my leadership challenges start with _____ !

    Most of my leadership changes start with _____ !

Review:

Five Thoughts About Modeling

1. It is easier to teach what is right than to do what is right.

2. People do what people see.

3. Work on yourself *before* you work on others.

4. Work on yourself *more* than you work on others.

    5) The example of _____ has profoundly influenced _____ .

Application

1. After whom are you currently modeling your leadership style? Why? Are you modeling what you are communicating as expectations to others?

_____

_____

_____

2. Does/did your model develop other leaders?

_____

_____

_____

3. What are you doing to build trust with your team?

_____

_____

_____

4. Are you open with your team, showing faith in them, encouraging them? How are you doing this? How would they answer this question about you?

_____

_____

_____

5. Are you answering "Yes" to the four questions you were given to ask yourself before you ask something from others? If not, what can you do to change the answer to yes?

_____

_____

_____

Put into Practice

In this session, most of the time was spent discussing modeling. Modeling is a very important step in the development of others as they will do primarily what they see. Think intentionally about how you are portraying yourself to your team and the individual you have chosen to mentor. Use a journal if necessary to log how you are modeling the leadership skills you want to develop. Set aside time to intentionally choose the traits you are going to model and develop. Make a list and review it daily.

DEVELOPING the LEADERS AROUND YOU

SESSION 4

SESSION 4

Review:

The Five Step Process for Turning Producers Into Reproducers

1. I Model

2. _____ _____

> *"Our chief want in life is somebody who shall make us do what we can."*
>
> —RALPH WALDO EMERSON

Two Questions for the Apprentice:

1) _____—Can he or she do what is required?

2) _____—Will he or she do what is required?

Two Questions for the Mentor:

1) _____—Has he or she had proper experience?

2) _____—Has he or she modeled excellence?

Two Questions for the Apprentice and the Mentor:

1) _____—Are they compatible?

2) _____—Is there mutual respect?

Characteristics of an Effective Mentor:

❖ _____, the wisdom that comes only with age

❖ _____, the ability to hear what another is attempting to put into words without judging

- ❖ Genuine _____ for others and their stories and their times— a respect that begins with reflection upon one's own story

- ❖ The ability to keep things _____

- ❖ _____-_____ , the willingness to share parts of one's own journey when appropriate and the willingness to be honest

- ❖ The ability to _____ a person's development level

People respond differently to development, and I have found from personal experience that each person who does grow will plateau at one of the six levels of development:

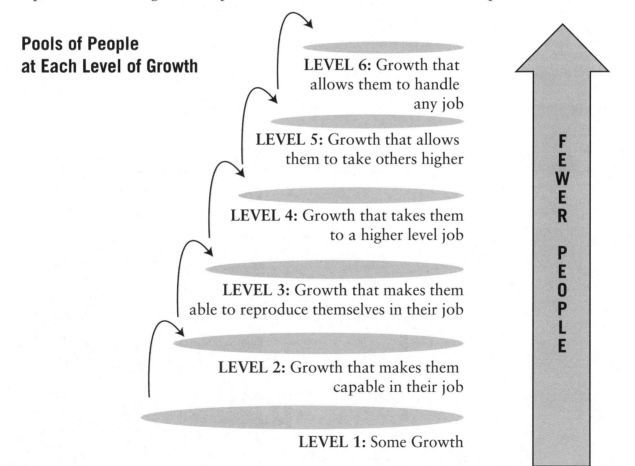

Pools of People at Each Level of Growth

LEVEL 6: Growth that allows them to handle any job

LEVEL 5: Growth that allows them to take others higher

LEVEL 4: Growth that takes them to a higher level job

LEVEL 3: Growth that makes them able to reproduce themselves in their job

LEVEL 2: Growth that makes them capable in their job

LEVEL 1: Some Growth

FEWER PEOPLE

—*Developing the Leaders Around You*, Page 126

SESSION 4, CONTINUED

Observations:

1. Levels #1 & 2 will possibly provide producers, but not reproducers.

2. Level #3 is where a producer becomes a reproducer.

3. Level #4 is a result of a person's growth potential and reproduction.

4. Level #5 is where a reproducer becomes a MVP.

Review:

The Five Step Process for Turning Producers Into Reproducers

1. I Model

2. I Mentor

3. ＿＿＿＿＿ ＿＿＿＿＿＿＿

Personal Success—

"Success is the maximum utilization of the ability that you have."

—ZIG ZIGLAR

Organization Success—

"Success is the maximum utilization of the abilities of those within your organization."

—JOHN C. MAXWELL

What Potential Leaders Need

1. **Handles**—This is when you distill truth into bite size principles that they can apply. All good mentors can put life lessons into a nutshell that is transferable.

   Question: "Is the apprentice 'fleshing out' these transferable principles?"

2. **Laboratories**—Another role is to provide a place where he can practice the principles he's learning in a safe place; you point them to where they can do it.

   Question: "Have I provided that 'safe environment' and is the apprentice taking risks?"

3. **Road Maps**—All good mentors furnish direction for life. These "compasses" or "roadmaps" provide options on how to best get to their destination.

   Question: "Is the apprentice following the 'game plan' and demonstrating creativity?"

4. **Roots**—This means you supply a solid foundation, from which a mentoree can build his life. It represents the stability and security necessary to grow and flourish.

   Question: "Has the apprentice demonstrated security that fosters growth?"

5. **Wings**—These represent the ability to see new horizons, then to enable the mentoree to fly and achieve beyond what they imagined they could have done alone.

   Question: "Does the apprentice realize that their development is a result of a mentoring relationship?"

—**Tim Elmore**

SESSION 4, CONTINUED

4. _____ _____

Evaluating Yourself as an Empowering Leader:

Put a number at the end of each question from 1 to 10. 1 = never 10 = always

1. Do I believe in people and feel that they are an organization's most appreciable asset? _____

   It's wonderful when people believe in leaders.
   It's more wonderful when leaders believe in people.

2. Do I feel that team leadership can accomplish more than individual leadership? _____

3. Do I look for potential leaders and quickly assimilate them into the organization? _____

4. Do I desire to raise others above my own level of leadership? _____

5. Do I invest time developing people that have leadership potential? _____

   Growth is NOT an automatic process.

6. Do I enjoy watching others get credit for what I taught them? _____

   *"It's amazing what can get accomplished
   if it doesn't matter who gets the credit."*

   —MARK TWAIN

7. Do I allow others the freedom of personality and process or do I have to be in control? _____

8. Do I give my influence publicly to potential leaders as much as possible? _____

9. Do I plan to have others take my present position? _____

10. Do I hand the leadership baton off to a teammate and truly root for him or her? _____

> **Go to the people,**
>
> Live among them.
> Learn from them.
> Love them.
> Start with what they know,
> Build on what they have.
> But of the best leaders,
> When their task is accomplished,
> Their work is done,
> The people will remark,
> "We have done it ourselves."
>
> **(Chinese poem)**

5. _____ _____

Levels of Leadership:

- ❖ Entry Level—Leaders _____ where they are going.
- ❖ Credibility Level—Leaders are able to take _____ there.
- ❖ Accepted Level—Leaders are able to take _____ there.
- ❖ Highest Level—Leaders are able to take _____ _____ there.

Equipping is a three step process.

1. _____ — _____
2. _____ _____ _____ — _____ _____ _____
3. _____ _____ _____ _____

Leaders should remind themselves of the words that Andrew Carnegie had inscribed on his tombstone: "Here lies a man who knew how to enlist in his service better men than himself."

SESSION 4, CONTINUED

Application

1. How are you including your mentorees in the process? Are you allowing them to come along side and assist you? Are you explaining not only the how, but the why?

_____

_____

_____

2. List some ways that you are providing growth opportunities for your mentorees. How are they progressing? Are you giving them encouraging feedback? Are you assisting them and correcting them in a positive manner?

_____

_____

_____

3. What are you doing to motivate your mentorees? What qualities in them do you reward?

_____

_____

_____

4. Are your mentorees beginning to model and train other leaders? Why or why not?

_____

_____

_____

5. What types of leaders are you training? Is it going as expected? Are you finding the right group of people? Are you putting them in the right places to be effective? What has been the result within your team?

_____

_____

_____

Put into Practice

In the final session, we discussed the final four steps for turning producers into reproducers. Now that you have modeled the way, it is time to take the next steps to training up your potential leaders. This will require you to have strong communication, respect, and trust. Make an agenda of what you will work on with your potential leader and stick to it. Don't overload them. Encourage them regularly. During the process you will be able to remove yourself systematically from the process so they are doing more and more themselves. Work with them on how to take another person on the journey. Finally, keep evaluating and soon you will have strong new leaders capable of developing others.

NEED MORE WORKBOOKS?
DO YOU NEED A LEADER'S GUIDE?

ORDER THESE RESOURCES ONLINE
AT MAXIMUMIMPACT.COM